WOODCHUCK

A Science I CAN READ Book

WOODCHUCK

by Faith McNulty

Pictures by Joan Sandin

Harper & Row, Publishers
New York, Evanston, San Francisco, London

It is winter.

The earth is cold.

In the cold earth
there is a hole.
Deep inside,
a woodchuck sleeps.
Her nest is made of
dry grass.

She has slept

for many months.

The woodchuck

has eaten nothing.

She has not moved.

Her body is quite cold,

but she does not feel cold.

She takes only one breath

every six minutes.

Her heartbeat is very slow.

Her deep sleep

is a special sleep.

It is called hibernation.

In the meadow

there has been snow

and freezing wind.

The grass turned dry and brown.

In the cold winter

there is no food for a woodchuck.

But she does not starve.

She goes down a hole

and sleeps.

She does not need food.

In a deep sleep

she lives safely through the winter.

Early spring comes.

The sun shines on the meadow.

It warms the brown grass.

The woodchuck moves a little.

Her heart beats faster.

She breathes more often.

Her body trembles.

She is getting warmer.

She is waking up.

Slowly she uncurls.

She yawns.

She leaves the nest.

She goes upward to the sun.

She goes up the long tunnel

to the meadow.

She looks out of the hole.

The sun is bright.

She smells the fresh wind.

She hears the cry of a bird.

Now she is awake.

She must look for food.

A few weeks pass by.

Each day the sun is warmer.

More birds come.

Each day the woodchuck

comes out to eat.

She finds new green buds

in the dry dead grass.

Often she stops eating and looks up.

She looks and listens for danger.

One day she hears a bark.

A dog is coming toward her.

The woodchuck runs.

Her legs are short.

She cannot run as fast as the dog.

But she has a head start.

The dog chases her.

The woodchuck reaches her hole.

She dives in and goes down.

The dog sniffs the hole.

He barks.

He digs.

But he cannot reach her.

After a while he goes away.

The sun is warmer.

The woodchuck is by her hole.

She is dozing in the sun.

Suddenly the wind brings

a new smell.

She sits up.

A small, brown animal is coming.

Quickly she dives into the hole.

But she doesn't go down deep.

She turns around near the top.

She waits there.

She makes a chattering sound.

It means she is excited.

The brown animal

is another woodchuck.

It is a male.

He is looking for a mate.

He smells the hole.

He smells

the female woodchuck.

He pokes his head down the hole.

He makes a chuckling sound.

It is a woodchuck greeting.

The female chatters at him.

She is not friendly

to strangers.

She rushes up the hole.

But the male will not go away.

Slowly, slowly, he crawls

close to her.

His tail is flipping up and down.

He stretches out his neck.

His nose touches her nose.

She does not bite.

She sniffs at him.

Then she goes slowly

back down

the hole.

The male follows her.

At the bottom of the hole

they mate.

The male stays with the female.

They sleep side by side

in the nest.

They nibble each other's fur.

The female is pregnant.

Her babies will be born

in a few weeks.

As the time comes near

she changes.

She wants the hole all to herself.

She jumps at the male.

She chatters with anger.

The male tries to nuzzle her.

She chases him away.

The male goes off by himself.

He will never see his children.

Four woodchucks are born.

They are tiny.

They have no fur.

Their skin is pink and wrinkled.

Their eyes are closed.

Their mother noses them gently.

They make very, very tiny

crying noises.

They crawl along their

mother's belly.

One baby finds a nipple.

He sucks and gets milk.

Soon all the babies find nipples

and suck warm milk.

Four weeks pass by.

The babies grow.

Fur covers them.

Their eyes open,

but it is dark in the hole.

They can see nothing.

They can feel their mother.

She is warm.

Whenever they are awake

they find a nipple and suck.

But the mother must eat, too.

She goes up to the meadow.

When she goes,

the little woodchucks cry.

They try to follow,

but the hole is too steep.

They crawl back to the nest.

They fall asleep in a heap.

Two more weeks pass by.

The little woodchucks are bigger

and stronger.

One day, when the mother leaves,

one little woodchuck follows.

The mother calls from the top

of the hole.

The little woodchuck answers.

He gets to the top.

He sees the sky.

He sees grass growing around the hole.

He sees sunlight.

He feels warmth.

He has met the world.

Soon all the little woodchucks

go above the ground.

They stay close to the hole.

They stretch out in the warm sun.

They begin to play.

They nibble each other.

They wrestle.

They roll on their backs.

They chase each other

in small circles.

But their mother does not forget
to watch for danger.
Every few minutes she sits up
and looks around.
If she sees something move,

she runs to the hole.

Soon the little woodchucks

learn to do the same.

One day the mother hears a bark.

She runs down the hole.

They run down after her.

A dog runs up.

He sniffs at the hole.

But all the woodchucks are safe

inside.

The little woodchucks look like
their mother.
They have short tails
that jerk when they are excited.
They have short legs
Their front paws look like hands.
They have strong claws to dig with.
They have sharp, curved front teeth.
Their teeth are good
for cutting plants.
Their ears are small and round.
Their eyes are dark as raisins
and they shine.

The little woodchucks have
long whiskers.
Their whiskers help them
feel their way
around the long, dark hole.

The woodchucks are bigger.

They want more food.

But their mother

has less milk for them.

They see her eating clover.

They try it.

It tastes good.

The mother goes off to eat.

The little woodchucks do not follow.

They are afraid to go far

from the hole.

They search for tender plants nearby.

They are learning

to feed themselves.

One day, the mother and the young
are eating in the meadow.
They enjoy the sun
and the taste of fresh greens.
One little woodchuck has gone far
from the hole.

Suddenly there is a bark.
It is very close.

All the woodchucks run.

The mother goes down the hole.

Three little woodchucks go down
the hole.

But a dog has caught

the fourth woodchuck.

The dog grabs her in his mouth.

He shakes her from side to side.

Quickly the little woodchuck is dead.

The dog carries her away.

Spring is over.

The sun is hot.

Daisies and clover bloom.

The three little woodchucks

discover that the flowers

are good to eat.

They find plenty to eat.

They are getting fat.

They are getting so big

that they do not fit in the nest.

46

It is time for the family
to break up.

The mother digs three new holes.
She puts each young woodchuck
in a hole of its own.
Then the mother leaves.

The young woodchucks are lonely.

They miss their mother.

They come out of their new holes.

But they do not know how to find
their old home.

There are sweet plants and clover
nearby.

They begin to eat.

Soon they feel better.

When they are full
they go into their new homes.

They fall asleep.

The next day
the mother goes to each hole.

She visits the first
young woodchuck.
They greet each other
with woodchuck sounds.
They nibble each other.
She leads him to the meadow.
There they eat, side by side.
After a while
they go back to the hole.
When he is safely in the nest
the mother leaves.
Again the little woodchuck is alone.

But this time he is not so lonely.

Then the mother goes to each

of the others.

She nibbles their fur.

She eats in the grass

with each one for a while.

Then she leaves them.

The young woodchucks learn

to live alone.

The days are hot.

The grass is tall.

Now the mother woodchuck

cannot see over the grass

when she sits up.

Insects are beginning to sing.

There are thunderstorms.

The young woodchucks stay

in their holes when it rains.

The mother does not visit them

in the rain.

53

Now the mother does not visit

the young ones every day.

On some days she forgets them.

And they forget her.

They are not afraid

to wander alone.

The mother visits each young one

a few more times.

Then, one day, it is the last time.

She will come no more.

Now each young woodchuck

is on its own.

The little woodchucks stay

in their holes for a few more weeks.

Then, one by one, they move.

Their short legs take them

a long way.

The smallest woodchuck
moves first.

She goes across the meadow.

She comes to a stone wall.

She stops and digs a hole.

Another woodchuck wanders

in a different direction.

He comes to a highway.

He starts to cross.

A car comes and he is killed.

The third woodchuck

goes up a sunny hill.

He finds

a hole under a bush.

It is empty.

It becomes his new home.

Autumn comes.

The woodchucks are busy.

They must eat a lot of food
and get fat.

Their fat will keep them alive
during their winter sleep.

The two young woodchucks

get bigger each day.

They are almost as big

as their mother.

They are fat, and their fur shines.

They are beautiful woodchucks.

There is a frosty night.

In the morning

the mother woodchuck

comes out of her hole.

The grass is cold and wet.

It has a silver shine.

The air smells cold.

The sun is pale.

It does not warm her.

She eats awhile

and then she goes to her nest.

She curls up in her nest

in the dark.

She goes to sleep.

When she wakes up

it will be spring.